DENALI
NATIONAL PARK

mt. mckinley

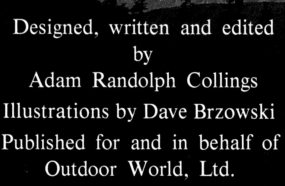

Designed, written and edited
by
Adam Randolph Collings

Illustrations by Dave Brzowski

Published for and in behalf of
Outdoor World, Ltd.
by
ADAM RANDOLPH COLLINGS
incorporated

Box 8658 Holiday Station, Anaheim, California 92802

Color separations and printing by Frye & Smith, Ltd., Costa Mesa, CA 92626
Special thanks to Jeff Bohman and Robert Butterfield of the National Park
Service for their invaluable assistance in preparing this publication.

Cover: Majestic DeNali "The High One" (photograph by Bill Possiel)
Title Page: Dall Sheep Ram (photograph by William K. Almond)
Opening Spreads in order: Polychrome Pass (photograph by Ed Cooper).
Reflection of DeNali, North America's highest peak, in a tundra pool
(photograph by Ed Cooper). Taiga forest (photograph by Ed Cooper).
Caribou, the American Reindeer, dwarfed by the glaciated slopes of
DeNali (photograph by Marilyn S. Hartley).
This Page: At 20,320 feet above sea level the slopes of DeNali are the first to
capture the rays of the morning sun and the last to succumb to evenings
shadows (photograph by Bill Possiel).
Last Page: Dogsled demonstration (photograph by Bill Possiel).

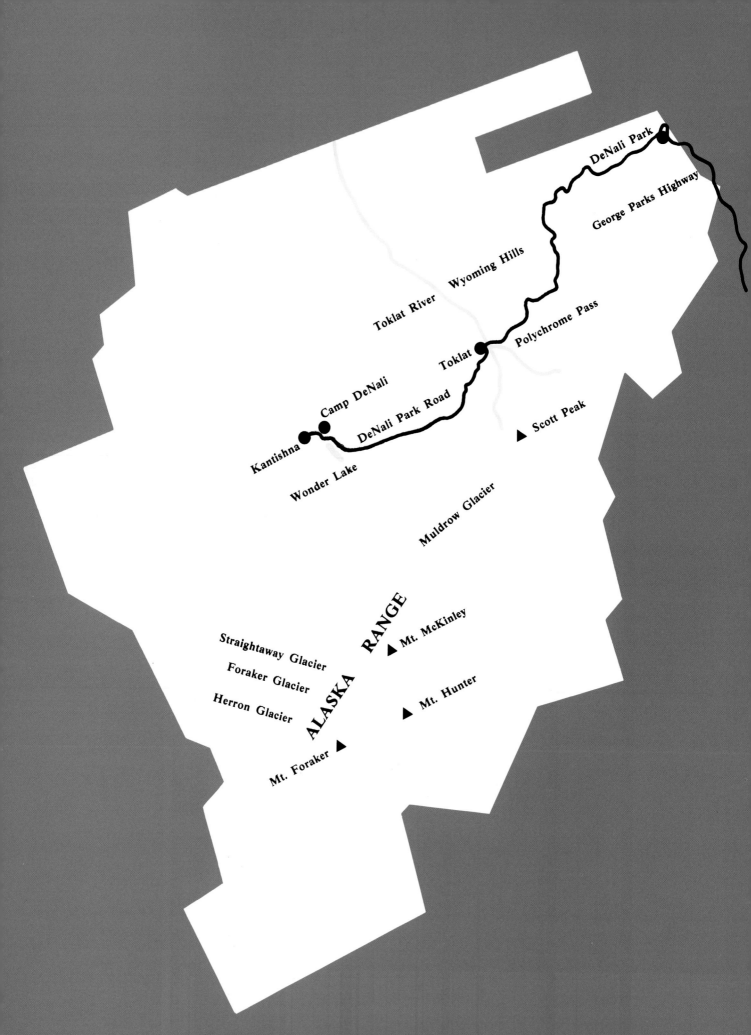

DeNali Park

George Parks Highway

Wyoming Hills

Toklat River

Polychrome Pass

Toklat

Camp DeNali

DeNali Park Road

Scott Peak

Kantishna

Wonder Lake

Muldrow Glacier

ALASKA RANGE

Straightaway Glacier

Mt. McKinley

Foraker Glacier

Herron Glacier

Mt. Hunter

Mt. Foraker

DeNali National Park

mt. mckinley

DISCOVERY:	Undetermined
SET APART:	By an act of Congress on February 26, 1917.
LOCATION:	South Central Alaska. The Alaska Range running along the southern border of the Park forms a geographical boundary line or barrier between coastal Alaska and regions of the state's interior.
SIZE:	6,000,000 acres.
DESCRIPTION:	Perpendicular mountains and glaciated high country – wooded foothills – vast expanses of tundra.
FEATURES:	20,320 foot high Mt. McKinley, highest summit in North America - ultrascenic Wonder Lake - extensive wilderness areas - teeming populations of big and small game including grizzly bear, moose, caribou, wolf, and Dall sheep.

Until the close of the last glacial period, some 10,000 years ago, great beasts such as the woolly mammoth roamed over the steppes and tundra of DeNali National Park (Painting by Zdeněk Burian).

DeNali National Park

mt. mckinley

In the midst of Alaska's great arctic wilderness stands a massive, ice-sculpted mountain unparalleled in both height and grandeur by any other such monolith on the face of the earth. Formed eons ago, this ancient shrine reaches skyward to surpass even the Himilayas, at the steepest vertical incline of any such mountain in the world.

Stresses beneath the surface of the planet had already buckled and warped the face of the land before the last great Ice Age set in, nearly a million years ago. Shifting continental plates initiated mountain-building activity that resulted in the birth of the Alaska Range.

As arctic winds began to blow across North America, great rivers of ice, glaciers, buried the landscape, flowing sluggishly across a frozen continent. Giant beasts, the woolly mammoth, cave bear, and mastodon, thundered over tundra that had once been marshlands and tepid inland seas.

Alaska's great mountain stood shrouded beneath snow and glacier. Dwarfed by extensive sheets of ice, it appeared as if but a mere island floating in the midst of a frozen sea.

Glaciation gave way ten thousand years ago. General warming trends fashioned the climate with which we are familiar today. Preserved in permafrost beneath the frozen northland, remains of such bizarre creatures as the woolly rhinocerous and saber-toothed cat remind us of a prehistoric world that only recently came to an end. Stark landscapes in America's Alaskan wilderness bare silent testimony to the powerful forces of Nature that sculpted our environment just prior to the dawning of modern times.

Crowning this Ice Age splendor, at 20,320 feet above the level of the sea, stands the stately mountain, in all her glaciated granduer--highest summit on the North American continent. Once locked in ice, the great escarpment now towers free standing above a vast expanse of tundra and

Cornice on summit ridge of Mt. DeNali.

taiga, forming an impressive capstone for the six hundred mile long Alaska Range.

To the American Indian this giant stone god was known as DeNali-"The High One". Nearby Mt. Foraker became recognized as spouse or companion to the mighty DeNali. Both were revered as dieties.

Maps drafted by early explorers of the "northern mystery" denoted "great ice peaks" and "distant stupendous mountains" on the vast unknown spaces they attempted to define. One such record spoke of a "cloud-like summit, far in the interior," a summit that could only have been "The High One" itself.

Russian occupation during the early 19th Century did little to open the interior of the Alaskan frontier. Outposts were confined primarily to the coasts. There, interests focused upon whaling operations and the lucrative business of harvesting sea otter pelts.

Discovery of gold on the Klondike brought to Alaska a sudden influx of Yankee fortune seekers. Subsequent acquisition of the Arctic territories by the government of the United States found the great mountain DeNali renamed McKinley in recognition of a future president's stance on the issue of the gold standard. The original name bequeathed this grand monument has persisted among the native Alaskans, however, and was recently recognized by Congress accordingly. Today that first christening remains intact.

As what is today one of the largest National Parks in North America, this, the highest eminence on the continent, has come to suggest somewhat of a symbolic focal point for wilderness preservation movements throughout the world. Here in the shadow of "The High One" modern man rediscovers his affinity with nature. We come to recognize the very essence of wildness--the beginnings from which we ourselves sprang. Stripped of the burdens inherent with our complex, urban society, we are herein free to escape via a virtual door that opens to us a scene once duplicated in most every corner of the globe. Lord grizzly reigns supreme over the land. Wolves, alone and in packs, scout the tundra and forests for prey. Great herds of caribou roam free to follow predetermined migratory routes as they have done since time immemorial. Giant moose amble about common environs with the small, spry fox and weasel. The mighty wings of the Golden Eagle course through an unbroken horizon. Spindly spruce, miniature birch, and a myriad of brightly colored wildflowers, in their season, clothe the land. There is no sign of civilization here; no semblance of industry or modern technology--only Nature's handiwork--the land, the flora, the fauna,--and rising above it all, the great mountain; visible from most every vantage point within the Park.

The idea of preserving wilderness for wilderness' sake was born in an era of exploitation by, oddly enough, perhaps the worst group of offenders the earth has ever known. Brash, assertive Yankee opportunists, in step with the philosophy of their day, perpetrated every scheme of profiteering imaginable upon the virgin frontier of their adopted homeland. Before resources were depleted, however, some among them became aware of the fact that once gone, certain elements of their natural world would remain lost forever.

At the very height of America's Industrial Revolution a cry for preservation went forth amongst the people. There was the voice of John Muir echoing across the nation from California's Yosemite Valley, and the watchword of Henry Washburn demanding protection for the Rocky Mountain's extraordinary Yellowstone Country. Far-sightedness stayed the forces that would have, if left unchecked, stripped America of her rich natural heritage.

To the cause of the Alaskan wilderness came a most unlikely mouthpiece from, of all places, New England; a gentle, civilized country, worlds removed from the Alaskan frontier.

A gentleman's gentleman, Charles Sheldon, born in Vermont, had been polished and refined by a strict Eastern upbringing. Accustomed to the finer things in life, his childhood in the mountains of his homestate had nonetheless fostered within the boy an intense sense of wonder about the natural world. During his youth he became an avid outdoorsman. Later welcomed into the ranks of New York's exclusive "Boone and Crockett Club" his activities led him to many exotic and faraway hunting grounds. Sheldon's keen sense of interest in the Alaskan wilderness was born on one such expedition in 1906.

That almost spiritual connection between the man and his destiny with "The High One" is best captured by the words of Sheldon himself, who revealed through his sketches and anecdotes a sensitivity rare among the sportsmen of his age.

"December 26. Morning temperature 31 degrees below. It was my purpose to spend this day about the base of Denali. Fog hung low when I rose before daylight, and although it continued, I started up the river bed. On the snow-covered moraine wolverine tracks were everywhere abundant, and old moose tracks were plentiful among the stunted willows along the river and elsewhere for three miles above the timber. After proceeding four miles I found myself above the fog. Denali, immaculately clear, towered above me, its lower slopes crossed by a thin band of pink vapor, the sky above it pink, yellow, gold, crimson, of everchanging color tones. Conies were bleating all about on the moraine, and willow ptarmigan were abundant. A chickadee flitted among the uppermost willows, and old tracks of a small band of sheep, coming from the outside mountain to the west, crossed the moraine toward the eastern foothills.

Great avalanches continually kept falling with crashing sounds that rolled among the outside ranges. The river near the glacier was open and the murmur of its current was audible though subdued. The whole vast

Charles Sheldon (right) photograph courtesy of The National Park Service.

Rich in history, the Alaskan frontier embraced within the boundaries of DeNali National Park still sports rustic sourdough cabins (right) and an occasional food cache (below) elevated to protect the mountainman's provisions from marauding bears. Once the only viable method of transportation in this land of long winters and deep snowdrifts, the dog sled (below right) is still employed. Demonstrations of this unique mode of locomotion are presented daily to the delight of Park visitors at the DeNali National Park Hotel.

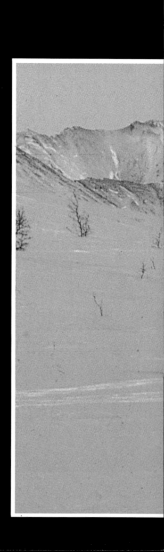

north face of Denali was mutilated by avalanches, exposing the underlying black rock. The great mountain rose above me desolate, magnificent, overpowering. The lower ranges were white, while below, nothing could be seen but the fog, which took on the appearance of thick clouds. I felt, as never before, completely alone in the presence of this mighty mountain; no words can describe my feelings."

Charles Sheldon, 1906

A consuming interest in studying wildlife together with a passion for big-game hunting caused the physically robust and ardent adventurer to reflect upon what might become of the abundance about him if left vulnerable to exploitation. The idea of creating a National Park that would encompass DeNali with its teeming population of animal life was born of that contemplation. Articulate as he was, he became Alaska's most vocal advocate in a campaign thus begun to set aside a treasure of wildlife and resources for the benefit of future generations.

At the time most seemed amused with the idea of partitioning off a section of wilderness within a wilderness. Somehow the concept took upon itself an aura of redundancy. Avid support from Sheldon's influential colleagues at the Boone and Crockett Club, however, added credibility to his scheme and clout to his fervor. On February 26, 1917 the dream became a reality, with an act of Congress that designated parts of the mountain massif along with the great valley to the northwest as a preserve for native wildlife.

Civilization's accelerated encroachment upon the American scene has since proven the wisdom of Sheldon's foresight.

Almost immediately the push for expansion of the newly created preserve began. Aided on its way by the thorough studies of Adolph Murie, a gifted and respected naturalist, the Congress of the United States was impressed and eventually persuaded to redefine and vastly enlarge the scope of Sheldon's experiment.

Murie's argument seems clear and simple to us now. Yet in the day that it was first raised it, like that of Sheldon's, seemed impractical and unnecessary. Murie wrote . . .

"The national park idea represents a far-reaching cultural achievement, for here we raise our thoughts above the average, and enter a sphere in which the intangible values of the human heart and spirit take precedence. Mingled with the landscape of McKinley Park (as it was then so named) *is the spirit of the primeval . . .*

All the plants and animals enjoy a natural and normal life without human restrictions. Freedom prevails–the foxes are free to dig burrows where they will; to hunt ptarmigan, ground squirrels and mice as the spirit moves; and they share in the ownership of the blueberry and crowberry patches. The grizzlies wander over their ancestral home unmolested; dig roots and ground squirrels, graze grass, and harvest berries according to whatever menu appeals to them. The "bad" wolf seeks an honest living as of yore; he is a respected citizen, morally on a par with everyone else. His hunting of mice, ground squirrels, caribou and Dall sheep is his way of life and he has the freedom to follow it. No species of plant is favored above the rest, and they grow together, quietly competing, or living on adjusted composure. Our task is to perpetuate this freedom and purity of nature, this ebb and flow of life–first, by insuring ample park boundaries so that the region is large enough to maintain the natural relationships, and secondly, to hold man's intrusions to the minimum."

Adolph Murie

Murie gave to an urbanized and far removed public a world with which they were unfamiliar; a world which, nonetheless, through his vivid descriptions and reports, fascinated them. His book "The Wolves of Mt. McKinley", published in 1944, is considered a classic in the field of natural history. The following selection from Murie's observations exhibits both his ability to educate as well as to entertain . . .

"On the flat the wolf stopped for a moment, and so did all the caribou . . . Then the wolf seemed to come to a decision, for he started after twenty-five cows and calves farther from him than those he had been chasing. Before they got under way he gained rapidly, but soon they were fleeing.

For a time the race seemed to be going quite evenly, and I felt sure the band would outdistance their enemy; but I was mistaken. The gap commenced to close, at first almost imperceptibly. The wolf was stretched out, long and sinewy, doing his best. Then I noticed a calf dropping behind the fleeing band. It could not keep the pace. The space between the calf and the band increased, while that between the calf and the wolf decreased. The calf began to lose ground more rapidly. The wolf seemed to increase his speed a notch and rapidly gained on the calf. When about ten yards ahead of the wolf, the calf began to veer from one side to the other to dodge him. Quickly, the wolf closed in and at the moment of contact the calf went down. I could not be sure where the wolf seized it, but it appeared to be about at the shoulder. The chase had covered about five hundred yards and the victim was about fifty yards behind the herd when overtaken."

Accordingly in 1980 as part of the Alaska Lands Act an additional 4,000,000 acres were added to the Park, including the formation of a new preserve, that would maintain intact the hunting grounds of the wolf and the rangeland of the caribou.

A National Park comprised of nearly 6,000,000 acres, DeNali, like the mountain itself, stands as a giant among wilderness preserves. As in the famous parks of Africa, this great legacy abounds in wildlife. A single road penetrates the Park, leaving the entire region virtually unintruded upon by man. Unprecedented encounters with species of North American game since extinct elsewhere are unquestionably the highlight of any guest's visit to the Park. Such a state of wildness demands, however, that all visitors recognize their position while in DeNali's domain. They are strangers here. As they roam about Park trails it is wise to make deliberate attempts at being both seen and heard so as to avoid undesirable encounters with startled grizzly or spooked moose. Author-photographer Aubrey Stephen Johnson related one such incident for the National Geographic Society, as he and his wife spent a leisure afternoon exploring the park.

"As I turned, peering downstream for my wife, two piercing screams told me where to look. Marilyn was crouched against the edge of a steep, upward sloping bank, arms covering her head, her back toward a huge honey-colored grizzly approaching at a rolling run.

To me the bear seemed to be upon her when suddenly it pulled up, throwing sod and gravel frantically as it changed course. Marilyn's screams had evidently transformed an attack into headlong flight. As the sow ran by me and crashed through a willow thicket to rejoin her fleeing cub, she looked very tired. I heard her breath coming in ragged sobs, with the tongue and teeth plainly visible through the open jaws. I have never seen a more frightened animal.

Marilyn, untouched though the bear had passed only three feet from here, recalled her moment of terror: "I knew that any second I would feel the claws in my back. I was in complete panic, and squatted where I was."

Evidently the bear had been betrayed by its weak eyes into believing that something

MARILYN S. HARTLEY

*other than human was near, and available
as prey. A strong wind had kept our scent
from her, and the roaring stream muffled
our sounds."*

By adhering to the obvious precautions, DeNali
National Park affords visitors with a unique and
most rewarding wilderness experience.

Generally speaking the DeNali Park landscape
can be divided into three basic categories, with
corresponding lifezones therein characterized. The
first, and most obvious of these "zones" would be
that of the mountains themselves. Encompassing a
large segment of the Alaska Range the animals
and plantlife of this great divide are restricted if not
prevented entirely from existence in a foreboding
realm of extreme conditions. Much of this region
remains buried year round beneath an irregular
sheath of snow and ice. Such ice flows form a
mantle that may extend hundreds of feet in depth.
Numerous glaciers radiate from the peaks of the
Alaska Range, which itself forms a virtual barrier
between the costal lowlands and Alaska's northern
interior.

Romping gingerly about the base of this
awesome landscape are the snowy-white Dall
sheep. Considered by many to be the most
beautiful animal anywhere, this handsome herbi-
vore is at home in DeNali's mountain fastness
where few elements threaten their security.
Surefooted, they gracefully scale the precipitous
slopes of the high country, leaping 12 to 15 foot
chasms with ease, to browse on alpine grasses
and flowers. Imposing headgear and piercing
gold eyes adorn each ram, who may weigh as
much as 200 pounds at maturity. Ewes and
yearlings keep to themselves except during
rutting season when dramatic displays of strength
are exhibited as the males challenge each other
for mating rights.

Due to DeNali's subarctic location, timberline
in the park occurs between 2,500 and 3,000 feet,
as opposed to the 10,000 foot delineation
encountered in the Rocky Mountains. Here
below the peaks and summits, nestled in the
foothills of the Alaska Range we encounter a
different environment; one denoted by the
Russian word "Taiga" meaning "land of little
sticks". Indeed such are the woodlands encountered within the park boundaries. Spindly spruce
and dwarfed aspen account for the diminutive
term. Most trees stand no higher than a moose.
Others crouch low, hugging the ground as a

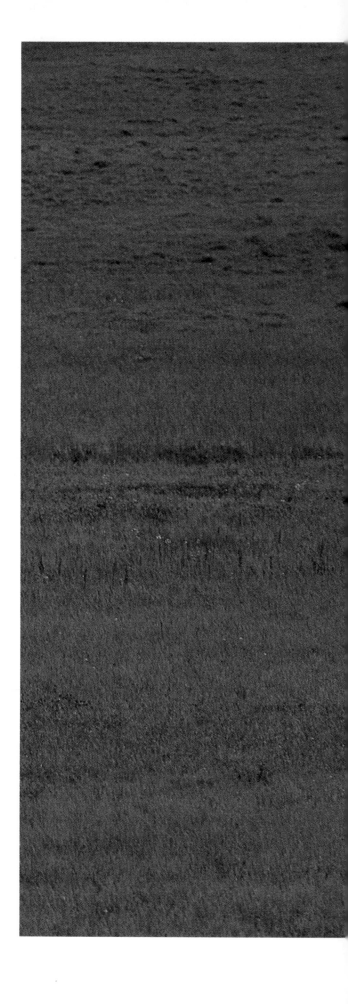

MARILYN S. HARTLEY

protection against facing the brunt of severe winter storms. It is here in this miniature forest that one encounters much of DeNali's wildlife population. Although caribou find the shelter herein afforded as desirable winter quarters to be abandoned at the first sign of spring, moose on the other hand prefer to make of this habitat a permanent residence. Lynx, wolves, and other predators tend to establish their dens in such areas, as do countless other varieties of birdlife and small mammals.

Stretching beyond the woodlands is the realm most typical of DeNali National Park--that of the tundra--an open prairie-like land stretching as if a carpet of green to russet hues against the vast, uninterrupted horizon.

Composed of numerous varieties of shrubs, sedges, mosses, herbs, and lichens, this third lifezone so dwarfs the individual as to be found quite as overwhelming and impressive as the great mountains themselves. Here man towers above the landscape, yet disappears in its vastness. Herds of caribou summer here as do the wolf packs that pursue them. Seven different species of voles and lemmings busy themselves constructing intricate networks of tunnels and

burrows beneath its mottled surface. In this realm the shrill alarm of the arctic ground squirrel or parky (he is so called because of the fact that his furs are used to make parkas) is a familiar sound. Grizzly bears, who, when quick enough enjoy dining upon the parkys, are often seen amidst the tundra; mostly employed in the business of gorging themselves on berries and roots.

Sanctuary for man in this wilderness haven is encountered at the entrance to DeNali National Park where stands the hospitable DeNali Park Company Hotel--an unusual structure constructed around a collection of railway cars; cars from trains that once served to transport visitors from neighboring Anchorage and Fairbanks (still a popular method of getting here). Nearby Mt. McKinley Chalets offer complete resort facilities. Elsewhere throughout the preserve excellent campgrounds and picnic facilities are provided by the National Park Service.

Shuttle bus and tram service allow access to the many natural features of the Park, with continuous daily service throughout the summer season. Although operations are limited in winter, snowshoe hikes, cross-country ski touring, and dog-sled trips enhance one's visit to the Park.

Summer's brief visit (June to August) is a popular time for hiking and backpacking. Would be mountaineers should be sure to take along their raingear, warm clothing, and plenty of insect repellant. Unstable weather is the only constant in DeNali while tundra turf plays host to more than 30 different species of mosquitos.

In a park such as DeNali public attention is naturally brought to rest upon the masterful art of mountain climbing. Each year a select few make the ascent to the top of "The High One" with the aid and under the direction of park service experts and up-to-date monitoring facilities. All modern conveniences considered, the climb remains a dangerous pursuit, reserved for those who can produce appropriate medical certificates and biographical sketches to substantiate their claimed skills and qualifications.

Earliest attempts at scaling the mighty massif were unsuccessful. A few reports of "gold-rush" contemporaries who professed to have conquered the mountain have been difficult to substantiate.

It was probably not until 1913, when a four man party directed by Harry Karsten, guide and

Reynard, as medieval minstrals called him, is a sly creature indeed. Masterful at the art of alluding pursuers, the red fox also distinguishes himself for his bravery, often risking death in attempts to divert danger from vixen and pups.

wilderness companion of Charles Sheldon himself, completed a successful climb to the roof of North America. Karstens' own account of that triumphant moment carries with it an exhiliration and zest that has thrilled and inspired countless other climbers and arm-chair mountain men since.

" . . . after we had relayed everything we wanted up to the glacier we broke camp leaving one tent pitched and proceeded up the glacier to very near 8000 ft. level, about 5 miles above where we first struck the glacier and here is where I had to solve the problem of glacier travel . . . I had to figer out bridging crevasses, good snow from bad snow. Ice bridges Natural & home made, it surely is some interesting . . . from the 8000 to 9000 there was a large serack to go over ft. shere from top of ridge to top of snow with many crevasses on it ranging from a foot to 50 feet wide, some were open and others covered with light drifted snow a slight touch and it breaks through. we would sprinkle snow on them till strong enough to bear blocks of snow & build an arched bridge which would hold like a stone wall. other places we would find blocks of Ice which had broken off and fallen half way across which would serve as a bridge. then emagin the grim Icey ridge on eather side with hanging glaciers discharging ice every few moments . . . 11500 the head of the Muldrough & the foot of the great N.E. Ridge which leads up to the upper basin between the two peaks. "O" it is a great sight a great basin a mile wide with towering cliffs on all sides but down the glacier, and a low saddle 500 ft. high in the N.E. ridge all covered with hanging glaciers and the great Ice falls coming out from between the two peaks and dropping ice a shere 4000 feet every 15 or 20 minutes. sometimes a great mass would break loose from a spur of the North peak goodness knows how many thousand feet . . . here is where we had our worst weather. we camped here three weeks, again & again Walter & I tackled the ridge, fogs & storms would drive us back and every time we went we had to shovel steps out . . . you can hardly emagine what a proposition that ridge was . . . when we tackled it it was a

MARILYN S. HARTLEY

BILL POSSIEL

MARILYN S. HARTLEY

WILLIAM K. ALMOND

Penetrated by a single highway the vast expanse of DeNali's wildlife refuge lies virtually unintruded upon by man and his machines. Shuttle and tour buses transport guests into breathtaking landscapes and exciting confrontations with Alaska's abundant population of big game.

RICK McINTYRE

ED COOPER

WILLIAM K. ALMOND

Clinging precariously to the slopes overlooking Polychrome Pass (below) or snaking through an early snowfall (below left), the drive through DeNali National Park is an unforgettable experience-left best to the skilled services of the shuttle and tour bus drivers provided. At Stony Hill Overlook (left) drivers turn interpreters as they share with park guests stories of the mighty mountain that stands before them.

PHOTOGRAPHS: RICK McINTYRE

Ranger guided "discovery hikes" (above and right) afford newcomers the opportunity of familiarizing themselves with the Alaskan frontier. For those who prefer their "discovery" experience be of a more individualistic nature, outstanding guides and maps are provided at any of the Park Service Visitor Centers. Either adventure merits the accompaniment of one's camera, as DeNali National Park, with its varied wildlife and spectacular mountainscapes, is a photographers "paradise".

BILL POSSIEL

Among the Park's most elusive wildgame, beautiful, snowy-white Dall Sheep (these pages) are perhaps best viewed through binoculars or telephoto lens as they ramble the precipitous recesses of the high country.

"Even without (the mountain, the park) would be outstanding because of its alpine scenery, its arctic vegetation, and its wildlife. I have walked over the green, flowering slopes in the rain, when the fog hid the landscape beyond a few hundred yards, and felt that the white mountain avens, the purple rhododendrons, and the delicate white bells of the heather at my feet were alone worthy of our efforts."

– Adolph Murie

ED COOPER

RICK McINTYRE

From nearly every vantage point DeNali, "The High One" (left) towers above tundra and taiga at the steepest incline of any mountain in the world. One begins to grasp the immensity of this giant monolith when it's compared to companions such as Mt. Hunter (standing to the left of DeNali in the photo below) whose own summit peaks out at 14,580 feet above sea level.

Family camping is a favorite activity at most
national parks. DeNali is no exception. Excellent

In sharp contrast with the overwhelming grandeur of the Alaska Range, DeNali National Park abounds in a myriad of subtle beauties hidden but for the chance encounter or the wary eye. The capricious melody of the songbird, the splash of rainbow color after a summer shower . . .

PHOTOGRAPHS: BILL POSSIEL

. . . the skittering of an arctic ground squirrel (parky) or ptarmigan in the tundra . . .

ED COOPER

MARILYN S. HARTLEY

BILL POSSIEL

. . . awaken the senses to an intricate world adorned
graciously by Nature's loving hands.

WILLIAM K. ALMOND

WILLIAM K. ALMOND

MARILYN S. HARTLEY

The beaver makes its home in park streams and ponds, where it busys itself throughout the summer constructing dams and hutches.

jumbled up mass of ice, Knife edge in places . . . blocks of ice in others. some balancing on the ridge, 2 blows of my axe sent one as big as a two story house crashing and roring into the basin thousands of feet below . . . cutting the top of the ridge off to make a path with almost shere drops on eather side untill we found a fairly flat place on the ridge at 13000. here we first used our small tent and oil stove. for five hundred feet above us it was terrably jagged and torn and then a sharp clevage up onto a snow slope which lead to the 15000 foot level and here was the hardest and most dangerous of them all getting up onto this snow slope, it was 50 ft. shere from top of ridge to top of snow slope and no chance of cutting steps up, so I cut down the base of the clevage along some drifted snow, every once in a while cutting a good foot hold in the ice so in case the snow gave away there was something to hold to . . . we gained the snow slope and found it rather steeper than we suposed but easy going compared to what was behind, after climbing up the snow slope (cutting steps all the way) about 1000 feet we where driven back by a storm, but next day we made the 15000 foot level, the edge of the upper basin. we were above the storms, the next two days we spent in relaying our camp and provisions up . . .

The next morning after we made camp at 18000 was a fine one. none of us slept that night. we pulled aut at 4 A.M. and reached the top at 1 P.M. Fine clear sunshinie day & a stiff wind blowing, thermometer recorded 4 above and it was some cold . . . we pitched a little tent I made for to read the instruments in. read the instruments, said a little prayer, erected a cross, took a few Photos, looked around a little and started down. 1 hour & 1/2 was all we

Adorned in chestnut red cape, a willow ptarmigan poses for the photographer.

BILL POSSIEL

The caribou, or American Reindeer warily roams DeNali's tundra. Airfilled hair coats, worn over thick body fat, help to provide warmth needed to survive harsh Alaskan winters.

WILLIAM K. ALMOND

Legendary predator of North America and undisputed monarch of the wilderness, DeNali Park's population of wolves is one of the few such concentrations left undisturbed on the continent.

ALAN CAREY

BILL POSSIEL

Triggered by a biological clock of sorts within the bear itself, Mother Grizzly and her siblings step up their feeding habits, gorging themselves on roots and berries, storing up much needed fat, that will enable them to endure the rapidly approaching winter months of famine.

ALAN CAREY

At McKinley Chalets (left) and DeNali National Park Hotel, a structure ingeniously constructed from rail cars (below) outstanding guest facilities are provided for the comfort of Park visitors. Regular air and train service from Anchorage and Fairbanks make of this wilderness an easily accessible getaway vacation resort.

PHOTOGRAPHS: BILL POSSIEL

could stand it . . . We reached the top of the Mt. on June 7, 1913, 1 P.M. and reached our base camp June 9th 10 P.M. What a change the smell of flowers & green things, every thing in summer bloom, it is hard for me to express. we laid over in base camp one day to clear up than packed dogs & our selves & started for Eureka which took two days in pouring rain. when I seen Hamilton I yelled for coffee & mush & plenty of it with lots of sugar and got it. I nearly foundered myself. I has lost 20 lbs. on trip . . .
Harry Karstens

In the portfolio herein we have attempted to capture, as best a publication can, the experience that is DeNali--the enormous vistas together with Nature's intricate network of sublimities--that we might be able to share with you ". . . this great banner of a mountain with its heraldic display of wildlife . . ."

Perhaps the mystery of the great North is best exemplified by the beautiful Aurora Borealis that adorns her evening skies.

BILL POSSIEL

THE END

ADAM RANDOLPH COLLINGS
incorporated